# A Way with Horses

# A Way with Horses

Understanding the horse and human relationship

Trudy Nicholson

The Lyons Press
Guilford, Connecticut
An imprint of The Globe Pequot Press

First Lyons Press edition, 2005
First published in New Zealand in 2004 by Tandem Press
First published by Random House Australia in 2005

The Lyons Press is an imprint of The Globe Pequot Press

10   9   8   7   6   5   4   3   2   1

Cover and text design by Nick Turzynski, redinc.
Photographic support and assistance Chaz Foxall Photographic Design
Printed in China

ISBN 1-59228-835-9

This book is not an instruction manual or a how-to book. No responsibility can be accepted for individuals'
interpretations of the author's text, nor for the ability of the person/rider, the equipment used and the
environment in which the horse is worked.  There is no quick fix or way to install knowledge.  It is my advice to
anyone wishing to work correctly with the horse to seek out a competent trainer, attend clinics and courses and
read; there is so much to know about the species; the learning process is ongoing.  Last but not least, nothing
surpasses the knowledge learned by spending time in the company of the horse. *Trudy Nicholson*

Library of Congress Cataloging-in-Publication
Data is available on file.

To my sister Sue – for giving the horse a voice.

# contents

# acknowledgements

S pecial thanks to Julie Ward Thorpe for her ongoing support during the writing of this book, for being there and assisting me with the editing and text.

I would also like to thank Steve Houston and Jody Hartstone for taking the time out of their busy horse-training schedules for photographic sessions; Chas Foxall for his photographic assistance, his technical skills, advice and support; Dr Jeffrey Grimmett, my work colleague, with whom I spent many working hours in the presence of horses, for his initial encouragement to take the first steps of this journey; Trudy Nicholson, my namesake and friend from the other side of the world, for her ongoing belief and encouragement to follow my dream. To my publishers Helen Benton and Bob Ross of Tandem Press for giving me this wonderful opportunity – thank you.

I would especially like to mention Simone Frewin and Hayley Booth for their giving so much time to be photographed with their equine companions; Vicki Mathison, my friend and colleague who encouraged my photographic career;

my long-time friend Denise Cook who gave time in the development of this project; Rosemary Aimers who introduced me to horsemen such as Jim Briggs and Steve Houston, who have since started several of my horses. Thanks also to Antoinette Crowther; Bella Reid; Kath Faulkner; Rae Grace; Lyn Murray; Jenny Connor; Kay Hogan, St Peter's School, Cambridge; Liz McIntyre; Liz Brown; Annette Knight; The Oaks Stud; Amber Crowther; Marilyn Jenks; Abby Lawrence; Juliana Cox and Annette McFadgen who in varying ways supported me during the making of this book.

I wish to thank the numerous horse owners who have so generously given their time during the photographic sessions. I want to thank my beautiful models – equine and human – both in New Zealand and overseas.

And last but not least a special thank you to my family, friends and teachers who have helped and supported me in my quest for the horse.

Trudy Nicholson

# introduction

T he horse has accorded us the astounding privilege of becoming part of the equine social structure. As always, with privilege comes responsibility, and it is that responsibility that I feel I owe to 'the horse' to pass on what I have learned over the years from horses I have shared my life with, through both my childhood and adult years. In this book, I present to you images and observations gathered throughout those years of being amongst this incredible species. I invite you to share with me in the journey the foal makes from his birth, life in the herd and beyond, to his introduction to being handled by humans.

The time the foal spends with the mare is relatively short in comparison with the time he shares in human company. For the horse, domestication can lead to a lifelong friendship with his human companion; both human and horse benefit when we make the effort to learn the horse's 'language'. However, the horse is part of an often misunderstood species; even by those constantly in his company, the basic instincts of this free-spirited creature are frequently misread. Many appear unaware of the basic fundamentals of horsemanship. So often the

horse is kept for our recreational, financial or personal use with little thought given to his emotional needs, and most of all his natural instincts. The horse is seen by many as a flighty animal – but this is only part of what he is.

This is not a training manual as such. It is a demonstration and a celebration of a wonderful way of being with the horse, and an appetiser to tempt you into experiencing it for yourself. This book is about that journey which the horse makes from the mare (his mother) to us, and in my photographic images I have captured the essence, body language and social interaction of the horse – all of which we need to understand in order to have a harmonious relationship with our equine companion.

This book is timely because in this decade of 'horse whispering' there is a growing awareness of a more gentle way of doing things; people are beginning to want to understand the equine language, with many questioning the logic of the old-style breaking-in procedures – now thankfully (if still too slowly) becoming outdated. The whole process can be introduced without pain or undue force, and with new words to explain the process, known by some as 'starting', it can be one that need not be stressful or dangerous to horse or human if the equine language is better understood. This, put quite simply, is the foundation of good basic horsemanship.

I do not claim my ideas are at all original or revolutionary; they have been around for years in various forms. They are, however, confirmed by my own observations and experiences of what horses have taught me, along with many human teachers and clinicians, in my quest to learn a better way of being with the horse. The photographs have been taken over the long periods of time, in different parts of the world, that I have spent in the presence of the horse, observing and learning from this magnificent, living, feeling creature.

It is my pleasure to invite you to come with me, on my journey, into my world of the horse …

**NOTE**: For ease of reading I refer to horses generally as 'the horse' and 'he', especially during the training process. The use of 'horseman' refers to both male and female. I also refer to the *breaking-in* process as *starting*. I prefer the word 'start' to the word 'break', which has negative connotations.

# new life

In the dark of the night she lies down to have her foal. The other horses in the herd are at rest. The birthing process is quick, in anticipation that the predator may be near. Within minutes the new life appears.

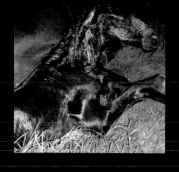

*I have only been in the* *a short while,*
*but instinctively I* *to get* *of my*
*legs and feet. After several attempts I manage*
*to* *. I seek sustenance from my*
*mother's milk...*

She softly nickers at the newborn foal beside her. She licks him to stimulate his circulation and responses. Already in survival mode, he fights to get up onto his feet. He takes his first steps and seeks sustenance from his mother's milk. Within a day, he can walk, trot and canter at her side. They move in unison – to the onlooker it is as if there is an invisible thread that connects them. His neurological maturity and unique leggy design enable him, even at this young age, to keep up with her in the security of the herd, lest he become easy prey for a predator.

He follows her example and flees as she does should danger approach. The horse's lightning-quick responses, athletic physique, respiratory system and stamina have equipped him for speed – all geared up to outrun his predators.

*...and before long I am able to                      ,*
*as if joined, beside her.*

'I *dance*, I *challenge*,
I *investigate*, I **play**...
I *find new* **adventure**
*and* I **gallop**.'

*...venturing out on my          , all under the watchful eye of my          who calls should I venture          .*

He is becoming aware of his surroundings and over the next few weeks he explores his world. He works at playing. As his confidence builds he wanders further from his mother for longer periods. He starts to interact socially with other herd members and, full of his own importance, he challenges them as he tests his boundaries. He is already learning about herd hierarchy. His mother, instinctively on the lookout for danger, calls to her young offspring should he wander too far. He has acute hearing and he is always ready to respond to her call.

# herd interaction, hierarchy and behaviour

The horse's main concern and purpose in life is to survive and reproduce. The wild horse's nomadic lifestyle enables him the freedom to travel any place over any distance as may be required to meet his dietary and physical requirements. Being herbivorous, he has no need to hunt. By and large a peaceful creature, he prefers a leisurely life, and spends most of his time in a leisurely way, picking at grass all day long, rolling, playing and galloping with other herd members.

He enjoys being socially interactive and with his mate enjoys the calming effects of mutual grooming. (As part of the human–horse herd, he may enjoy the relaxation he feels when his groom, with the body brush, massages his body – may even reciprocate by rubbing with his muzzle the groom who is providing such pleasure. It is said that mutual grooming releases endorphins, which give the horse a pleasant, relaxing sensation.)

He rests often, standing and dozing, relaxing a hind leg. Everything about him is designed for survival. Sometimes he stretches out on the ground, and while sleeping, another herd member – dozing with eyes open – looks over him.

In the wild the mare might let her foal suckle from her for up to two years. During this time the foal learns from the examples of the adult (his mother) he spends so much of his day with. His physical as well as psychological growth is being developed, and not unlike the human child, this young creature is learning acceptable behaviour and boundaries. He needs to feel safe. He learns where safety lies and where he should not venture. He learns protection and the security of being within the confines of the herd to which he belongs. He learns respect within the equine herd, as he learns about the pecking order and submits to superior members – often exhibited by mouthing, the suckling reflex, with an audible noise. As a six-month-old foal, although being socially interactive with other foals and horses, he still needs and heeds the reassurance and protection of his mother and herd.

When he becomes a yearling and then moves into the two-year-old stage (his adolescent phase) the colt can become quite bold. Colts (more than fillies) tend to exhibit their boldness, often standing on their hind legs play-fighting with other colts in the herd. When handled at this age, inhand he may exhibit similar behaviour and the human may find him quite difficult to control when on the end of the lead rope, especially in the hands of the unskilled.

Often acting coltish (exhibiting stallion-like behaviour) he may become insubordinate. He may be disciplined like the disobedient teenager he is. He may be sent to the outside of the herd and forced to stay there for some time until his attitude changes.

He is thus made to feel the consequences of his bad behaviour: alone out there, he is easy prey for the predator. Without the security of the herd (safety in numbers) he feels alone, insecure and under pressure. His life, in fact, is in danger. He feels the leader's powerful glance, and the need to conciliate, and wants to return to the sanctuary of the group.

When he shows signs of a changed attitude his request to return to the herd will be answered. The mare, by reading his body language, can tell when he has done his time, and may allow him to come back into the herd. She relaxes her own body language hence releasing the pressure he's feeling from her. He turns his head and faces her, focusing on her, confirming the signal to rejoin his family. He is pleased when he feels the release of pressure and is able to hook back into the security of the herd.

In the years following he becomes independent

of his mother and may be driven out by the stallion,

or wander off to form a band of his own.

In the wild the foal may stay with the mare

until he is an adult horse, often with his brothers

and sisters.

With human intervention the social

structure of the herd is altered and we even

become part of it.

# the human–horse herd

Until recently, we needed the horse more than the horse needed us. In the wild, horses herded together in an interdependent social structure perfectly suited to their survival. We, having discovered what multiple benefits could accrue from the domestication of this animal, found many needs met: transport; the carrying of burdens; the hunting and carrying and cultivating of food; the more efficient waging of war; even entertainment.

In today's consumer society the horse accommodates us well, but he can be dispensed with if, for whatever reason, we no longer require him. Bred for specific purposes, the horse's conformation and temperament are manipulated. We can choose whichever type, size and breed we so desire. With artificial insemination, the mare's perfect mate can even be chosen from the other side of the world.

The sheer speed and stamina of the horse is just one of the aspects that make him so attractive a possession to us. This is reflected in the quality of the bloodstock and other racing fraternities.

Take, for example, the controlled thoroughbred-breeding regime; the mare is valued for her fertility, her reproductive capacity calculated and charted, her foaling carefully timed for convenience, her pregnancy monitored and her progeny valued for their pedigree and earning potential. With carefully matched lineage, an equally fast stallion will serve the mare. The whole breeding process becomes very different to that of their wild counterparts out on the ranges.

Thoroughbreds have become earners of high stakes and consequently over the years have been bred for even greater speed. In this phase of his evolution the shape of the modern day thoroughbred has changed anatomically to allow the slanted hindquarters to power the horse forwards even faster than his predecessors. As with many breeds of horse, over the years, humans have altered the anatomy of the horse to accommodate our needs.

The horse is a commodity.

Indeed, nature seems to have been turned upside down in the

overall relationship between human and horse, but historically it

worked because of a complex interplay of mutual benefit. The horse

relinquished his freedom in return for security, freedom from threat,

and regular nourishment. We undertook those responsibilities and

in return benefited from the many ways the horse could assist us in

our daily lives and those of our communities.

" ...when they lose their environment
(i.e. the prairie) they die out – except
where man has chosen to domesticate them
because they were useful to pull ploughs,
for making war... They are not so necessary
now; just used for entertainment for
affluent human society, and easily
dispensed with when times get tough.
So therefore they are vulnerable in terms
of long-term survival as a species... "

Dr Jeffrey Grimmett
Equine veterinarian

‘ That small light face – vulnerable,
complex, bewildered, surrounded by
unidentified human forms – is so
expressive, so complete as a statement,
so compelling, that it pulls me into the
image with wrenching clarity. ’

*Trudy Nicholson*
*USA illustrator of nature books*

# 'My new relationship is with humans.'

The unhandled horse instinctively wants to flee if he feels

we are threatening him. In time he can learn that far from being

a violent threat, we can be partners in a relationship of mutual

trust. Such relationships with horses have been part of human

communities virtually since the beginning of recorded history.

The horse is, after all, a social animal.

# a silent language

Because the social life of the horse's family, the herd, depends on the sending and receiving of signals, we need to understand this equine language in order to communicate effectively and understandingly with the horse. By spending time observing the horse we will learn to recognise this silent language. The way of the horse is subtle, and as one's eye develops, the horse's body language – initially indiscernible to the human eye – takes on new meaning.

There is no great mystery to the understanding of the horse's language – frequently referred to as 'horse whispering'. Anyone who chooses can learn this unique equine language

and once undertaken it will become a valuable

teaching acquisition when working with the horse.

By understanding the psychological factor – the way

in which the main focus of the horse is on survival,

where only the strongest will get to lead – and

recognising the importance of testing within

the herd by its members we can gain an

advantage by becoming the superior herd

member. Horses react this way to each

other in order to make sure that the

strongest, the most superior horse always

gets to the top, because it takes a superior, strong (both physically and mentally) horse to protect the herd. So by studying the way in which horses communicate with one another we can begin to see the ways in which the horse sees the world quite differently from us.

Many humans overlook these social grazing animals, failing to recognise the complexity and interdependence of their world and their relationships. Similarly, the horse is not really concerned about us; his main instinctive concern is to reproduce his species and survive.

When taken from his herd situation with its purpose and meaning into the world of domestication, the horse finds that we can often be inconsistent, making him feel alienated, and confusing him by giving conflicting commands and instructions and failing to understand the primary imperatives of his natural instincts. By making the effort to understand and respect the way in which the horse perceives the world, we will benefit when training the horse.

# unique –
# horses, too,
# are individuals

Each horse is born unique, just as each human is. They come in many shapes, many sizes, and with their own personalities.

Some are braver, more intelligent, more athletic than others.

Some people prefer to work with geldings or stallions than mares. The influence of hormonal cycles is important to a mare and calls for sensitivity and patience from her handler. Gelding the colt results in fundamental changes in behaviour because all the consequences of hormonal change are avoided. This is not so for the mare, who must deal with the fluctuations of mood and inconsistencies that are the inevitable result of her reproductive cycle. Her handler must recognise that she has different needs, which are a natural part of her being.

These aspects of behaviour should be taken into consideration when forming a relationship with the horse. An assessment of what is required from the new horse is a major consideration. The horse's maturity, size and natural ability all need to be considered in choosing the horse with the required prerequisites. Even though the acquired horse may fit the bill, there is no guarantee of the end result. The horse, after all, is an individual and should be assessed at various stages of his training programme.

Many horses today are bred not for their temperament, but to run faster, to perform and to look better than ever. Temperament, however, is also an important consideration, which should not be overlooked in acquiring or working with the horse. Just as in any relationship between humans, if the horse-and-human team is to work as one, it helps if they are compatible enough to be able to work together without conflict.

# domestication

In domestication the herd structure changes dramatically. It is now the human's responsibility to protect the horse, make him feel secure, and to feed him. He is now dependent on the human to feed him adequately – ensuring he is supplied with a correct balance to cover his dietary requirements, taking into account the amount and type of work the horse is kept for. His wellbeing and exercise regime is executed and controlled by the human who now gives him the equivalent of a membership to a health and fitness centre. He is worked out and fed according to his given regime. He may be boxed (stabled) for most of his days, whereas in a natural environment he may walk and graze for up to 60 kilometres per day.

Depending on the time of year or climate in which the domestic

horse lives, he may be let out into the field to run and graze. Often

on cultivated pasture where many natural plants are routinely

sprayed or otherwise removed he can no longer forage for the

weeds and herbs he would naturally delicately seek to balance his

equilibrium. He may be fed in large, carefully rationed amounts

at set times. His digestive system, designed by nature to receive

a constant yet controlled intake of grass and other roughage may

often be put out of kilter and he may even suffer from colic and

other gut disorders.

With decisions on feeding, exercise and socialising taken out of his control he may easily become overfed, under-exercised and overexcitable. A food imbalance in his system could lead to his becoming stroppy, and the trainer may even notice quite a change in his personality. This normally placid creature may now be a much-changed individual, even unruly, because he is feeling his oats. With a build-up of energy that has to be released, it may be unfortunate for both the horse and trainer if the only place he can expend it is when he is caught, lunged or ridden, or during the schooling session. Unfortunately the build-up is such that he may let loose in the form of bucking, rearing, bolting or other unacceptable types of behaviour.

It is unfortunate when such explosions occur, for he may be labelled naughty, uncooperative, bad, and may even become dangerous. He therefore requires a vent for his pent-up energy. In the freedom of his field he can gallop, kick and play to his heart's content – he has an outlet.

Another way in which the confined or deprived horse may reveal his sorry state is by exhibiting abnormal behaviour (known as stereotypes). He may even become quiet and withdrawn (shut-down), or display any of a number of other neurotic or physical symptoms. He is, after all, a free-spirited animal that wants nothing more than to feel comfort, freedom, a place to roll in the dust and to interact with his mates.

# the free spirit

The horse released in the field, free to gallop, buck, play and investigate is not deprived as much as his stabled counterpart. He can make some decisions for himself and his more balanced equilibrium will be brighter. Horses, like people, need mental and physical space. The horse is curious by nature and needs a certain amount of stimuli and freedom to explore, forage and make his own choices. The owner, making allowances, can minimise his level of deprivation; the modern-day horse can adjust and live a happy and relatively normal life. We can make his life more pleasant by gauging his mental state.

We can compare him to how he would naturally be, and make appropriate allowances – make him a place where he can act as normal as possible and yet enjoy being a domesticated animal. We can make some positive changes, make him happier by providing him with an appropriate paddock to graze, doze and roll in; by hacking out with him and socialising with him; by taking him on beach rides, trekking over the hills, paddling in the river; by allowing him to be a companion to us as well as to others of his own kind.

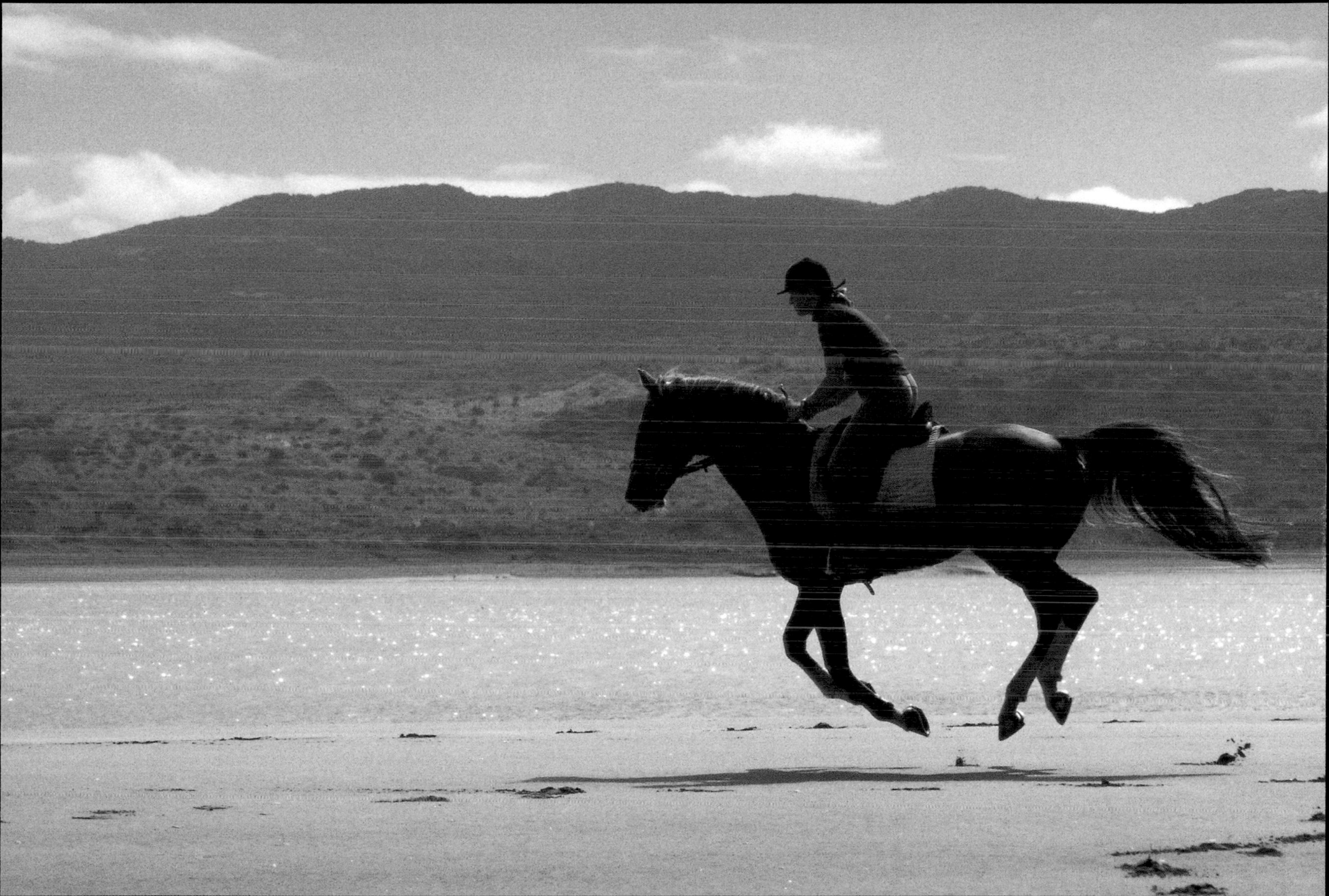

The horse paddocked alone can become dull and withdrawn, but he can also become overexcitable when out in the company of others. Although other species can be put with him to keep him company – such as goats or sheep – there is nothing like his own type. Always remember he is a herd animal. Like humans, horses do not like a life of solitude and boredom. We make most decisions for the horse. He has no choices over where or with whom he would like to be. The other extreme is overcrowding, when horses, unable to get out of each other's way in confined areas, may fight. The superior horse, normally requiring a larger area around him, can push the weaker horse out of his space as he takes the control. Negative, physical confrontations may result, causing injuries. Often, just as the new group is patterning out and when the horses are getting things

sorted, the human appears, causing jealousy or aggressiveness within the group. How often have you gone out to greet your equine companions and one turns on the other, ears pinned back, teeth baring as you approach? We have created a restrictive environment in which we expect the horse to conform and feel happy and contented. He focuses on his leader for survival – he now focuses on us.

We have a huge responsibility to make the horse feel secure. The relationship differs from that of the horse herd; the horse has accepted us as part of his herd and therefore now requires positive guidance by his new leader whether working, playing, or in the arena together. He needs to learn what is required of him and what is acceptable behaviour. Physically as well as psychologically the horse is now dependent on the human.

The head mare does not use physical torment to control the herd – neither then do we need harsh, physical restraints to have control of the horse. If this were so, how is it that the small girl can direct, reins flapping, her pony whilst doing a round of jumping? Or what about an elderly or fragile person trusting the horse that they ride in a therapy session? For the mare, having control of the herd is not a matter of harsh physical dominance; she has their respect and leadership.

By using this approach based on knowledge of equine psychology both human and horse will have a fruitful and trusting relationship in which mutual respect is a key factor.

# connecting
# with the horse

When starting with horses, there are advantages in using the tool of safe enclosure – the 'round pen' (corral). Within the pen, the horse can leave should he feel the need for more space. When first turned out into the round pen, the young horse (not unlike the colt who was sent to the outside of the herd) may feel a huge amount of pressure. The young horse in his new environment (the round pen) may feel insecure and unsure of his trainer's presence and may even feel he is being punished. The horse may also have major concerns

for his survival, and being unsure of this new unidentified figure in the middle of the pen may instinctively want to flee. Because he has the freedom to do this, he may set off in a gallop around the pen – feeling the release of pressure (freedom to run from danger) he can make choices: he has consequences for his actions. He may now make the transition down to the trot, inhale a breath and do a double take. He may then stand with ears pricked, looking, and given the time to digest the new situation may have a change of mind. The situation is altering and the horse, becoming more comfortable, may look to the trainer for reassurance; he may question where he fits into this new group.

With the situation still forming, and the horse feeling fragile, the slightest change in the trainer's stance or body language may set him in flight again. The language of both parties in this formative stage, although subtle, is effective. The horse, feeling less threatened (because he knows he can leave at any time), may lick his lips and shake his head, with nose stretched out, signalling his intentions of wanting to 'hook on' to the human. He may even turn his body and look at the trainer and may now take a step towards him. The trainer may approach the horse with all probability that the horse will not turn in haste. An exceptional process takes place – the horse has asked if he may join the human – the human accepts and the union is made.

*Familiar language...*

It is an indication that the horse now trusts the human – so

now the trainer has a huge responsibility not to break this conviction.

There are many terms for this marked moment between horse and

human, and it is unique as from this point on the whole relationship

changes. In this book, we refer to this observable fact as 'hooking

on'. There is no set way to write this or a 'how to do' list of

instructions as each and every horse and horseman are individuals

and each case needs to be independently assessed. Although a

physical as well as a psychological attachment, it happens within the

horse's mind – it is as if ropes do not restrain the horse yet he follows in the shadow of his trainer. The horse still has the freedom to leave (flee) from this psychological attachment should he feel too much pressure. The outstanding thing about this occurrence is that the horse now 'chooses' to stay. He does so because he feels comfortable, he feels safe, he feels receptive and he is now willing to be led (taught) – he follows (learns) with no strings attached.

Hooking on between the free-spirited horse and the human is a beautiful and special affair to observe. The horse is willing and receptive – just like a human in the correct learning environment.

# learning
# together

**W**hen the correct attitude and movement is reinforced, the
horse finds the comfortable way to learn and the progressive

training steps take place. The young horse then becomes more

receptive to the training procedure that follows.

In using the round pen as a tool, we have developed a way to communicate with the horse while at the same time allowing the horse the opportunity to leave should he feel too much pressure. The important aspect when working the horse is not the amount of pressure that is put on but *the timing of the release* of that pressure.

*Friend?*

The weanling looks to his trainer for some security as he contemplates the safety of the approaching halter.

Here the weanling is being introduced to unfamiliar feelings, sights and sounds.

The horse soon learns to find *comfort* with the trainer, becoming *accepting* of the new aspects of his life.

He then becomes *curious* about his new surroundings, seeking

*security* from his trainer and developing a *willingness* to learn.

On the back of this horse and in the hands of her father this

child, like this horse, knows only a relationship of trust.

# leadership, assurance and trust

Once the relationship is formed with a human partner, the horse, trusting his leader, will gladly follow and perform to his human partner's suggestions. This filters through to handling, riding and even to competition level. It becomes a 'partnership' of trust and the results may be deeply satisfying to both horse and human. Friendship, and the willingness to follow, shapes his whole attitude so that together they enjoy their shared activities.

❨ *Trust...* ❩

There are many things to take into account when working with the newly ridden horse. There are no set rules, because each horse is an individual and each stage has to be monitored as the training progresses. If rushed, the process will take a step back rather than forwards, because a bullied horse will become tense. Children do not learn under such conditions; it is no different for the horse, who is, after all, on a huge learning curve. He has much to give – and much is being asked of him.

If force is used – such as by the use of cruel gadgets or hard

hands – the focus is on one place, normally the position of the

horse's head, to force the horse to work in an outline. With the

incorrect use of his muscles he may become uncomfortable and sore

to the point that he will eventually not be able to work properly.

If he is experiencing pain, he may resort to bucking or bolting

as a response; with unjust treatment he has no other way of

communicating his dilemma. With such methods, the horse cannot

move correctly and this will become apparent at latter stages when

more advanced movements are asked for.

The horse must be encouraged to move forwards into even rein contact encouraging free movement, looseness of joints and suppleness, hence the use of his hindquarters. The building of the muscles does not come from the head back, rather the energy is propelled from the hindquarters forwards. The horse carries most of his weight on his forehand – his hindquarters act as his driving force, his engine as it were. That engine has to be fuelled.

The art of riding is the learning, and understanding, of how to do this. There are no short cuts to this process, and the success of each stage will reflect the way in which the horse is worked by his trainer.

He may be feeling some physical discomfort due not only to the unaccustomed use of his muscles but also to the weight of his rider. Like any other athlete, the horse has to be built up slowly. With the correct workout and training procedure the horse can develop physically and build his muscles in preparation for the work to come. The trainer, recognising the temperament and ability of the horse, will take these facts into account and ascertain what is best for that individual horse.

There comes a stage when the horse is asked to lower his head and *reach* for the bit. As the horse progresses he will be able to maintain a contact for longer periods, and as he becomes stronger he will be able to engage his hindquarters and work in a more collected frame. He will be able to maintain a rein contact for longer periods.

As he becomes stronger he will be able to carry more weight on his hindquarters, allowing the forehand, head and neck to be carried higher. Once he becomes accustomed to working in an outline, more advanced work can be asked for. He may be introduced to lateral work and other school exercises.

Softness of the back, accepting the bit and working in a round outline is asked for with soft giving hands, and impulsion asked for by the rider's legs, driving the horse forwards into an even contact. The horse is unable to move correctly forwards into hard brutal hands that pull against him – he will become confused by conflicting requests and will hollow his back, eventually ruining his physique.

As training progresses, the horse becomes better balanced. He starts carrying more weight on his hindquarters. The horse and

rider's centres of gravity come into unison; they begin to work as one. Their minds become more in tune with each other, the rider using his mind and the horse carrying out the manoeuvres. They become so in tune that the rider's aids become less visible and the horse carries out a movement as if reading the rider's mind. It is as if some invisible force unites them. Anyone who has witnessed the beautiful and true art of dressage will have noted how subtle the connection between horse and rider can be.

We can all strive for such heights of perfection. No matter what your goal is with your horse, it should and can be performed in harmony with him.

Whatever the end result is that you wish to achieve with your horse, whether it be showjumping, dressage or western riding, or simply pleasure and companionship, the basic principles apply. The

trainer's understanding will be the foundation for producing an

accomplished horse. The horse reflects his trainer. I noticed over the

years of competing how the same people would come out time after

time with different mounts, doing the same things, getting the same

results – sometimes good, sometimes bad. Whether this is positive

or negative the pattern seems to be formed and can only reflect the

way that person is with the horse.

So often the horse tries to tell us of his discomfort, fears and

uncertainty in the situation we have placed him in. Was the message

clear or conflicting? The confused, and often scared horse, unable to

interpret the human's requests, may lash out by bucking, bolting,

rearing and refusing to move forwards, or some other form of intolerable behaviour. The rider may feel anger or fear towards his horse, but it is more likely to be the horse feeling confused and scared. Fear, his main emotion, is again instinctively causing the horse to flee from or fight what is threatening him.

He has to learn what is acceptable, but we in turn have to learn and understand that his natural behaviours are triggered by his given instincts. Maybe he did not understand what was asked of him – was he given clear instructions? Did he feel safe? Had he been taken away from the security of his mates? Does he feel secure with his human's leadership? The horse needs consistent instructions and a trusting environment in which to work. A trainer can develop a working relationship without force.

The domesticated horse, often kept within the confines of his field, needs stimulation and outings – it is up to us to make sure he is not physically or emotionally deprived.

At first, excursions may be hair-raising for horse and rider, but as he adapts, with his confidence building, he learns to enjoy his escapades. He needs balance in his life – not just shows, work and schooling. He enjoys being hacked out and a gallop along the beach or trek through the forest – he is, after all, a horse. With conditioning he adapts well to new locations.

At first, when introduced to such new environments the young or inexperienced horse will constantly be on the lookout. Anything new that he cannot identify he may perceive as a lurking danger, because, for the horse, his strongest instinct – that of the prey animal – will always be alive within him. We have to accept this about the horse in order to understand him. It is not complicated or confusing, but a matter of accepting the way in which the horse perceives his world. With the right attitude, you can reassure the horse that nothing is going to hurt him.

So when he is first taken out to shows and other new places you can expect him to react quite differently to the way he behaves when at home in familiar territory. He may be overwhelmed by all the new activities that now surround him, his fear factor greatly intensified.

My rider allows me *time* to *explore* new things.

He may not understand why the same thing that scares him does not alarm you. He may nudge you to warn you, but because he is confident in you, when he sees there is nothing alarming you he will relax and tone down. If the handler or rider becomes tense, the horse may well sense this and reflect it in his own behaviour. Though out of line, his excitable behaviour should be ignored as much as possible for now so his trainer's reassuring stance can communicate itself to him to calm him. If given a little time to look around and absorb the new and exciting surroundings he will soon settle, realising that the supposed lions lurking in the show stadium do not really exist, and he will become more focused on his trainer again.

We may start and train and ride him, we may compete on him and trust in him, we may condition and desensitise him to the world in which he now exists, but no matter how well trained and adjusted he may become, his instincts are still those of a prey animal. He therefore needs to feel the security of a leader.

The masters liken working with a horse to a dance, with the human leading. The best teachers I have known have also been great leaders... They all had a few things in common; they approached things honestly and sincerely, with regard and respect for those they led. There was an air of confidence about them, yet they were compassionate, open-minded and remained composed in tough situations; they had dogged determination tempered with a sense of humour that allowed them to keep things in proper perspective. They were humble yet had the ability to inspire. There was never any question as to who was in charge and you found yourself willing to follow them anytime, anywhere and through anything. The key word here is willing, because you cannot develop willingness, respect and trust through force. It is no different with the horse–human relationship. There are very few natural-born leaders, but we can all strive to develop some of these qualities.

*Jim Briggs*
*Horseman, clinician and USA Pony Club examiner*

*'I perform to my partner's suggestions.'*

❮ *Partnership.* ❯

What a joy it is, too, that feeling of working at one, in harmony, with the horse – and what beauty to the eye, watching a horse working in unison with his rider, whatever the chosen discipline. You have progressed to the stage where your thoughts and actions become one and with instant timing the horse performs to your requests. The very things that can work against us can be turned around and used to work for us. The horse's quick reflexes and will to perform can be used to his ultimate advantage when performing in the arena.

'...on the cross-country he is so confident –
and I feel we could jump the moon!
We feel like a real team...'

*Kate MacKenzie*
*Event rider*

Top competition horses do not perform because they are

forced; their will to work is a result of skilled training. The horse

needs to be confident in himself and in his rider. Take a top

eventing horse; look at the way he focuses and listens to his rider's

guidance with quick reactions, knowing the rider will not ask

something he is not capable of. The rider's leadership is so strong

that the horse performs trustingly, giving his all, around a

demanding cross-country course.

# communication, respect and reward

Groundwork is an important place to start when working with the horse. Both academically and physically the understanding of groundwork needs to be established in order for the foundation to be laid. Every horseman knows you cannot give working with the horse a time limit. The horse will tell you when it is time to progress to the next stage. By observing his subtle signs – his body language – the way he tilts an ear, or breathes, his stance and so on, you will know when he is ready.

All of these signs have meaning. The experienced horseman reads these and within a short period of time is able to climb onto an unbacked horse.

A rider who looks at what motivates the particular horse he's working with can understand him better by evaluating him as an individual and will work and reward the horse accordingly. He judges when it is time to progress to the next stage. He takes it in small steps. He understands the body language of his equine friend – noticing his stance, whether the horse is feeling too much pressure – step by step a continual questioning and observation of how the horse is feeling.

The key, the fine line is the *timing* of the putting on and the *release of pressure*. The horse develops the understanding on the ground and, once understood, with the increased trust in his trainer,

the backing (riding) follows fluently. The newly backed horse is

already familiar with the language of his trainer and is receptive,

waiting for his new command; and because he is receptive, he

develops a willingness to learn. Instead of it being a matter of

force, quite the opposite occurs, with the horse waiting for his

next command. He *wants* to perform.

The intimidating size of the horse makes him an interesting

subject to work with; however, some people can feel overwhelmed

by his massive body mass. Overwhelmed by his size, and with lack

of understanding, people often shackle the horse into submission.

This is especially noticeable during the time of the 'breaking-in'

process. The horse is physically unable to defend himself, tied with ropes; the fight is taken out of him. This results in nothing more than a shut-down, lifeless being, or – the opposite – a horse that has learned to fight the human.

People who inflict such pain and suffering on the horse are nothing but bullies.

At the other end of the scale some people think that by being overly nice and gentle to their horse he will in return be good and sweet back. They anthropomorphise and put into their own words what they think the horse is thinking or feeling from the human's perspective.

It may be advantageous to take note that the horse does not rationalise like the human, nor does he have human intellect. Without respect for the human the horse can potentially be a dangerous animal.

'...[The] horse, being a herbivore, herd-type species, requires the protection from the group in that they buddy up and are very socially dependent and we now find the horse includes us in their social group. Not many species allow that to happen.'

*Dr Jeffrey Grimmett*
*Equine veterinarian*

Respect, however, does not mean a submissive, downtrodden, broken-spirited horse. In the natural herd situation, the respectful members of the herd are still lively and life-loving – not dull, withdrawn and listless creatures.

Sometimes when things are not going right during the training process the horse is labelled 'naughty' – more likely he just does not understand what is required. A useful analogy is to think of yourself in a foreign country where surrounding you are foreigners and customs you do not understand. You try to talk, but cannot make yourself understood. The foreigners respond in their language; between the two of you there is a conversation that is achieving little – conversation but not communication. You may feel frustrated and even annoyed. The situation becomes confusing. Sometimes you may make progress by the use of gestures or body language; you may break things down and simplify your request; slowly you make some headway. The foreigner responds to your request; although it may not be quite the right answer, for now it is progress. Now communication is beginning.

Using a basic approach based on knowledge of equine psychology with discipline, consistency, respect and trust, all horses can be soft, attentive and responsive. The aim is to produce calm, confident, obedient and well-mannered horses.

Just as humans generally relate positively to the security of clearly defined boundaries, so, too, do horses. Such boundaries are commonly the guidelines by which we order our lives. In a similar way, horses respond to signals and language which define the

acceptable boundaries; and provided our use of such signals and

language is consistent, clear and understandable, they will cooperate

to the best of their ability, to an extent that is almost awe-inspiring.

As any horse lover will confirm, the opportunity to enjoy such a

mutually respectful relationship with a member of another species

is more than just a pleasure, it is a privilege, and one in which the

effort and dedication it demands are amply rewarded.

'Long, happy road ahead...'

# about the author

Trudy Nicholson grew up with horses, attending pony club and competing as a child. Her love affair and involvement with the horse continued into her adult years when she became a teacher of horse riding, both to children and adults, bringing many through to competition level. She has trained show horses, competed in dressage at national level and worked in the thoroughbred

Her photographic skills and knowledge of horses give her the ability to capture the body language, relationships and emotions of the horse in a uniquely expressive way.

When not travelling to expand her photographic library, her base is a small rural holding in Nelson, New Zealand. This is her second book.